CELEBRATING THE FAMILY NAME OF NICHOLS

Celebrating the Family Name of Nichols

Walter the Educator

Silent King Books
a WhichHead Entertainment Imprint

Copyright © 2024 by Walter the Educator

All rights reserved. No part of this book may be reproduced in any manner whatsoever without written permission except in the case of brief quotations embodied in critical articles and reviews.

First Printing, 2024

Disclaimer

This book is a literary work; the story is not about specific persons, locations, situations, and/or circumstances unless mentioned in a historical context. Any resemblance to real persons, locations, situations, and/or circumstances is coincidental. This book is for entertainment and informational purposes only. The author and publisher offer this information without warranties expressed or implied. No matter the grounds, neither the author nor the publisher will be accountable for any losses, injuries, or other damages caused by the reader's use of this book. The use of this book acknowledges an understanding and acceptance of this disclaimer.

Celebrating the Family Name of Nichols is a memory book that belongs to the Celebrating Family Name Book Series by Walter the Educator. Collect them all and more books at WaltertheEducator.com

USE THE EXTRA SPACE TO DOCUMENT YOUR FAMILY MEMORIES THROUGHOUT THE YEARS

NICHOLS

In fields where oak and willow bend,

Where rivers twist and skies extend,

The name of Nichols takes its stand,

Rooted deep in heart and land.

Beneath the wide and open sky,

Where generations come and sigh,

A family, steady as the stone,

Their legacy is all their own.

The Nichols name, a quiet grace,

A story carved in time and space,

Of hands that work, of minds that dream,

Of strength that flows like mountain streams.

Through valleys green and pastures wide,

Where shadows dance and hopes reside,

They till the soil, they sow the grain,

Their toil as constant as the rain.

But Nichols is not just the earth,

It's love and laughter, joy and mirth,

It's firesides warm, where children play,

And elders weave the tales of day.

A name that echoes far and near,

That whispers courage, stills all fear,

From humble roots, they grew to stand,

Like towering oaks across the land.

The Nichols clan, both fierce and kind,

With wisdom deep and open mind,

They carry with them dreams untold,

Of futures bright and hearts of gold.

In every path their feet have trod,

They've built with faith, they've walked with God,

With values forged in light and storm,

A legacy both rich and warm.

Through trials faced, they've learned to rise,

With steady hearts and watchful eyes,

For Nichols, like the rising sun,

Shines ever bright, each day begun.

Their name is more than line or thread,

It's memories of lives well-led,

It's kindness shared, it's bonds made tight,

It's guiding stars in darkest night.

ABOUT THE CREATOR

Walter the Educator is one of the pseudonyms for Walter Anderson. Formally educated in Chemistry, Business, and Education, he is an educator, an author, a diverse entrepreneur, and he is the son of a disabled war veteran.
"Walter the Educator" shares his time between educating and creating. He holds interests and owns several creative projects that entertain, enlighten, enhance, and educate, hoping to inspire and motivate you. Follow, find new works, and stay up to date with Walter the Educator™

at WaltertheEducator.com